Show Me the Money!

Understanding the Value of Your Business

by

KUMI D. BRADSHAW, MBA, CBA, BVAL

ASGILL POST
www.asgillpost.com

www.kumibradshaw.com

Edited by Cindy Orticio
Illustrated by Mike Ferrin

ISBN: 978-0-9566106-0-7

For my parents, Michael and Edmina...

For my brother, Kieran...

For all my loved ones... past, present and future...

Thank you!

Contents

Introduction

As a business owner, you will face decisions that influence your company's direction, its health, and in some cases, its very survival. It is critical that you be able to recognize these moments, as well as process the available information and take appropriate action with both a short-term and long-term perspective.

This book is intended to serve as a primer for business owners, professional advisors, providers of financing, investors, and fiduciaries who make important decisions in areas such as raising and restructuring of financing, financial strategy, business purchase or sale transactions, and dispute resolution.

The material is presented in four parts:

1. **An overview of business valuation,** explaining how to choose a valuation professional, describing the different valuation techniques, and providing a quick back of the envelope calculation
2. **Tips and considerations for buying or selling a business**
3. **Business finance topics,** with a focus on cash flow, financing, and banking relationships
4. **Special circumstances in the business lifecycle,** including transitioning leadership to another generation, divorce, buy-sell agreements, and ESOPs

Reader's Note:

- The terms valuation professional, business valuation professional, appraiser and business appraiser are used interchangeably throughout the text and refer to the same person.
- For the purpose of brevity, the male gender is used as a default in the text. No gender bias is intended.

Part 1.
AN OVERVIEW OF VALUATION

What to Expect from a Business Valuation

There are numerous reasons why you may seek a business valuation or appraisal—the terms are used interchangeably. Reasons include sale of a business, development of a buy-sell agreement, or preparation for handing a business down to the next generation. What can you expect from this process? This chapter offers some considerations for choosing a valuation professional, reviews the process and the methodology, and comments on the final report you will receive.

Choosing a Valuation Professional

The skill and experience level of your chosen business valuation professional are key. The valuation professional will have to effectively manage the process—information gathering, communication with concerned parties, appropriate application of valuation methodology. Look for someone with the following attributes:

1. **Appropriate qualifications and training.** Your business appraiser should be experienced, trained, and appropriately accredited. Training should be specific to the valuation of privately held companies, as the methodology differs greatly from the valuation of public companies. Ask if the appraiser has been accredited by one of the major business valuation professional bodies. Also request a curriculum vitae/resume as well as references from past clients and/or sample work.

2. **An absence of bias and self-interest.** Your valuation professional should be like Caesar's wife: virtuous and above all suspicion! Professional competence and ability are one side of the coin; the other is for the appraiser to be impartial, independent, unbiased, and nonpartisan.

3. **Strong ethics.** Your appraiser should measure up to all professional and ethical standards.

4. **A logical, systematic, and detailed approach.** Given the critical nature and importance of the valuation process, the appraiser should

present an end product that is logical, comprehensive and valid, while also being lucid and easily understood by the intended audience.

The Process

Before commencing your engagement, your chosen valuation professional should be able to provide a clear roadmap, describing the steps to be taken. This roadmap should address details including your responsibilities, an initial information request list, an expected timeline, and approximate cost for the valuation process. Generally the process consists of six steps:

1. **Preliminary conversation.** The valuation professional will discuss case details with you, including the nature of the business interest to be assessed, the quality and availability of financial and other key information, the purpose of the valuation, expectations regarding timelines, and potential conflicts.
2. **Proposal.** Based on the preliminary information, the valuation professional will decide whether his company is an appropriate fit for the engagement. If the answer is yes, he will respond with a proposal outlining an understanding of your needs, a proposed approach, a timeline, an estimated cost, and an engagement letter containing the appropriate technical and legal language.
3. **Information request/assessment.** Upon your acceptance of the proposal and receipt of any required deposit, the valuation professional will provide a comprehensive document request checklist and will arrange, as appropriate, for a site visit and interviews with management.
4. **Valuation calculations/report draft.** The valuation professional will perform valuation calculations, assessing both the 'hard' financial data and the 'soft' contextual data relevant to the engagement.
5. **Valuation review.** The draft reports will be reviewed and, as appropriate, sent out for peer review.
6. **Delivery of completed valuation report.** The valuation professional will deliver the finished end product to you—normally in the form of a bound, valuation report.

Methodologies and Tools

Your valuation professional will have a number of tools available. The choice of tools will be specific to your individual case, but you can expect the applied methodology and tools to:

1. **Be contextually appropriate,** i.e., take into account both the 'big picture' and the specifics of the case.
2. **Be appropriate to the operating environment of your business,** i.e., account for economic, legal, business, local-specific and segment-specific factors.
3. **Include comparative strategies and tools** to evaluate the company/business vis-à-vis industry standards and similar competing businesses.
4. **Be clearly explained,** including support for his opinion.

An End Product That Meets Objectives

You can expect the end product—the valuation report—to have several attributes:

1. **A declaration** by the valuation professional that the report presents an unbiased, impartial, and professional opinion.
2. **A statement of assumptions and limiting conditions**.
3. **A description of the assignment**, including the valuation date, restrictions on the use of the report, the consideration being assessed, etc.
4. **A clearly stated opinion of value.** This may be a specific value or a range of values.
5. **Support for the opinion of value,** including the information considered, the appraisal approaches used, and the research and thought processes that support the appraiser's analyses, opinions, and conclusions.

Valuation Approaches and Methods Explained

Essentially, all appraisals to determine value have their basis in the principle of substitution, which states, *"The value of an item tends to be determined by the cost of acquiring an equally desirable substitute."*

There are two fundamental bases on which a company may be valued:

* As a going concern
* As if in liquidation

The appraisal concept of 'highest and best use' requires an appraiser to consider the optimal use of the assets being appraised under current market conditions. Business appraisal theory recommends that unless otherwise instructed, if a business will command a higher price as a going concern, then it should be valued as such. Conversely, if a business will command a higher price if it is liquidated, then it should be valued as if in orderly liquidation.

Overview of Valuation Approaches

Going concern value assumes that the company will continue in business and looks to the company's earning power and cash generation capabilities as indicators of its value. Appraisers use three traditional approaches when assessing a business:

* The market approach
* The earnings or income approach
* The asset-based approach

Under each approach, specific valuation methods are available for use. Appraisal standards suggest that an appraiser test as many methods as may be applicable to the facts and circumstances of the property being appraised. It is then up to the appraiser's informed judgment as to how the results will be reconciled in delivering a final estimate of value.

Market Approach

The market approach uses information from the transactions of comparable businesses or value parameters of publicly traded companies as a basis for estimating the value of a business. When applied to the appraisal of common stock, consideration may be given to the financial condition and operating performance of the business being appraised relative to those of publicly traded companies in the same or a similar line of business and subject to similar economic, environmental, and political factors. This method generally has limited applicability in appraising smaller closely held businesses due to the lack of reliable information concerning sales of comparable privately held businesses and the unavailability of comparable publicly traded companies that can be used as guideline companies.

Earnings (Income) Approach

The earnings approach, which is income oriented, assumes that an equally desirable substitute for the business being appraised is one that has similar investment characteristics. This approach involves estimating the level of normal continuing earnings of a business, determining the applicable relationship between earnings and value, and then converting the expected earnings into an estimate of value. Generally, the approach is based on either historical or future earnings, depending on whether historical earnings are considered representative of the expected future earnings of the business.

Oftentimes, industries have appraisal formulas that are used to estimate the value of a business. Usually, these industry methods are expressed as a rule of thumb such as a multiple of revenue, earnings, units, assets, or equity. Rules of thumb are not recognized as acceptable methods for professional appraisal purposes because every valuation engagement has unique attributes.

Asset-Based Approach

The asset-based approach is based on the premise that one form of an equally desirable substitute for the business being appraised would be a duplicate of the underlying assets of the business. As applied to the appraisal of common stock, the asset-based approach calls for the summation of the fair market value of each individual asset and a reduction of that aggregate by the total liabilities of the business.

The asset-based approach is generally most appropriate for appraising several types of closely held businesses:

- Businesses that are nonoperating, such as holding companies
- Businesses that do not have an established earnings history, such as start-up companies and businesses with highly volatile earnings
- Businesses that are not profitable or marginally profitable

The asset-based approach is particularly appropriate when the ownership interest being appraised has the ability to liquidate or sell the underlying assets of the business. Generally, the approach is not appropriate for appraising minority interests in a business.

Applicability of Approaches

The three approaches are not mutually exclusive but are somewhat interrelated. The appraisal process is composed of integrated, interrelated, and inseparable techniques and procedures designed to produce a convincing and reliable estimate of value.

It is important to note that the preliminary estimates of value may require modification to reflect the respective rights of the stockholders:

- A control premium may be applied when the ownership interest being appraised represents a controlling interest.
- A discount for lack of control may be applied when the ownership interest being appraised represents a minority interest.
- When the ownership interest represents the shares of a closely held business, a discount for lack of marketability may also be applied to recognize the lack of a ready market of buyers and the resultant lack of liquidity.

A Back of the Envelope Calculation

When first thinking about buying or selling a business, many people want a quick and easy way to gauge an appropriate price. However, they may not yet be ready to invest the time, effort, and expense needed to get a professional business appraisal done.

Using rules of thumb is a common practice for people who are trying to get a general idea of whether or not a business is priced appropriately. These rules of thumb predominantly look at a multiple of earnings. However, the specific multiples vary. There is a significant difference between buying a business at 3 times earnings vs. buying a business at 7 times earnings. Is the multiple appropriate for this business or for this industry? What if the profits change or need to be adjusted? Most importantly, can this price be justified in the marketplace?

Since most business purchase/sale transactions are financed externally, we suggest that you first look at the business from the perspective of a lender (such as a bank). How much would it lend for this transaction?

The Calculation

Assuming a fixed-rate loan, with equal, regular payments, a bank would consider the following:

- **Forecast net income.** The lender will first want to get a feel for the likely profitability of the business. A business with insufficient profits will be unable to service the required loan payments.
- **Coverage of the loan payment.** Most institutional lenders will do everything they can to protect themselves against bad loans. They generally require a margin of error with regard to the borrower's ability to repay the loan. For example, they may require that a borrower (who is paying only from what the business earns) generate sufficient profits after paying all other obligations to cover a multiple of the required loan payment.

- **Interest rate.** Borrowing money comes at a cost. Banks, which have their rates published on their websites, tend to charge less than individual investors, who may want a 'piece of the action.'
- **Loan term.** The term of the loan is the length of time the borrower has to pay back the money. The term of the loan allows calculation of the number of loan payments that must be made.
- **Loanable value.** Given the previous information, the loan amount that the business can support can be easily calculated using a loan amortization spreadsheet, using the future value function in your spreadsheet software or using a financial calculator.

Some Caveats

Some businesses are more attractive to lenders than others. Perspectives differ depending on the identity of the lender. For example, some local banks tend to prefer lending to businesses with real estate holdings and other tangible assets, while private investors may place more emphasis on other factors. Some lenders may be willing to make 'risky' loans where they are less sure of the business's ability to produce sufficient profits but they have sufficient security.

The rule of thumb is an inappropriate methodology for a professional business valuation. A professional valuation considers elements including:

- **Purpose and function of the valuation.** For example, the value of a business for sale is different than the value of a business for divorce purposes.
- **Whether the business is being valued in whole or in part.**
- **The type of industry in which the business operates.** The methodology used to value an asset-rich business such as a construction company or guesthouse would be different from that used to value a dentistry practice or advertising agency.

Part 2.
BUYING OR SELLING A BUSINESS

DON'T LEAVE
UNTIL YOUR
HOMEWORK
IS FINISHED

Buying a Business?
Do Your Research First!

I f you're thinking of going into business for yourself, then one of your first thoughts may have been about what sort of business to start. Entrepreneurship has its risks, but many of the challenges associated with starting a business from scratch can be leap-frogged by purchasing one that's already in operation.

So, how does one determine what kind of business to buy? Perhaps you heard about the business through word of mouth or the media or have had direct experience as a customer. You may even work as an employee of the business or for a competitor.

There are many options from which to choose, and the decision-making process can seem daunting. As with any large purchase decision (buying a house or a car, for instance), you have to conduct the proper research to make an informed decision. In other words, once you believe that you have finally found the 'perfect' business to purchase, do your due diligence.

Due Diligence

Due diligence is a structured research process that can be separated into three distinct stages: *identification, verification,* and *assessment.*

Stage 1: Identification

This is where you, as the buyer, identify what you need to know in order to make an informed and responsible decision. You'll also decide how you'll go about gathering the information, and how much information you'll actually need.

When assisting clients with due diligence, we start with a standard checklist. Five major areas need to be examined in most business purchase transactions:

1. **Details of what is being sold.** This is where you'll need to obtain documentation such as an asset list and details of agreements impacting future operations (including contracts and gift certificates). Basically, you'll want to know everything you will receive or become responsible for if you take possession of the business.
2. **Historical financial information.** This includes profit and loss (P&L) statements, balance sheets, bank statements, point of sale records, contracts, etc.
3. **Operations documentation.** How is the business currently operated? This includes manuals, customer lists, payment policies, and any other documentation you may need for day-to-day business operation.
4. **Employee and human resources information.** This includes information pertaining to employees and management, such as the background of key personnel, payroll lists, identification of those requiring work permits, and job descriptions.
5. **Details of existing and potential obligations that could be inherited.** These include government obligations (payroll tax, social security), outstanding accounts payable, potential lawsuits, and contracts.

Stage 2: Verification

In the verification stage of the due diligence process, you should ask yourself two basic questions:

1. Is all the information being presented accurate and truthful?
2. What am I missing? Is there additional important information that I haven't obtained?

One of the first things buyers, banks, investors, and others look at when evaluating a business is its financial history. This is important for determining the worth and future viability of the business. What did the company gross in sales last year? How profitable was it? Are there any noticeable trends?

Despite the relative importance placed on this information, a surprising number of private businesses, particularly small businesses, have inadequate financial records. Even when a business has complete financials prepared by a qualified accountant, records are often not independently confirmed. As a potential buyer, what should you do? We recommend enlisting the services of a professional with a strong background in finance, particularly entrepreneurial finance.

Stage 3: Assessment

Once the key details have been identified and you feel comfortable about the integrity of the information (having verified it independently), the focus should turn to evaluating whether or not your potential purchase makes sense. We recommend that you consider the following:

1. The general effect of a change in management/ownership
2. Your relationship with employees and customers
3. The capacity of the business to generate enough profit to pay down loans or other financial obligations
4. The time and lifestyle demands of the business
5. How much working capital will be needed to operate effectively
6. The potential effect of external factors including competition, changes in the legal environment, changes in customer preferences, and market changes
7. Your risk profile, strengths and weaknesses as a potential buyer and whether or not the purchase of this business is a good personal fit.

Keys to Success

Purchasing a business has its risks, but you can reduce the risk by conducting a thorough due diligence process. We recommend three keys for successful due diligence:

1. Use professional assistance where appropriate.
2. Communicate effectively with the seller, financing sources, and anyone else involved throughout the process.
3. Work efficiently, but do not rush.

Good luck, and Caveat Emptor!

Selling Your Business?
Know the Three P's

Did you just get into business last week? Perhaps you've owned your business for 20 years? It doesn't matter. Be prepared to sell it!

That's right—even if selling your business is the last thing on your mind today, you should understand the sale process and be well prepared for this possible endgame. For a better perspective on what it takes to get your company ready for sale and why it's so important to be proactive, consider the three P's of selling your business: planning, professional involvement, and preparation.

Planning

Advance planning helps to eliminate headaches and makes for a smooth transition. In an ideal world, new business owners would incorporate an exit strategy into their initial business plan. In reality, not many business owners think about their exit strategy until they have been approached, they are ready to sell for their own reasons or a merger/acquisition opportunity arises.

In the event that a potential sale is on the horizon, we recommend talking to a professional as soon as possible to discuss your options and plan your strategy. Which brings us to the next P of selling your business…

Professional Involvement

The process of selling your business is time intensive and can get quite complex. For this reason, you may be well served by enlisting the services of a business intermediary. And reduce distraction from ongoing operations.

A business intermediary can help leverage their experience in areas including buyer or seller representation, assistance with deal structure, management of the sale process, assistance with pricing the business appropriately, and more—all to facilitate a smooth and successful business transfer while reducing the risk of the deal falling apart .

Preparation

The scout motto *"Be prepared"* is particularly appropriate for business purchase/sale situations. Sometimes out-of-the-blue offers are made, with quick turnaround and desired transfer of the business in a matter of weeks. At other times, apparently attractive, appropriately priced businesses take as long as 12 to 18 months or more to sell, even though the buyer and seller had been in talks as soon as the business first came on the market. Here are several recommended preparatory steps for you and your management team.

Personal Steps

1. **Prepare emotionally.** When the time comes to sell your company, you may find yourself struggling with unexpected anxiety. Seller's remorse is not uncommon. Your sense of identity may be tied to your role in the business. Even more challenging from an emotional perspective can be a situation in which you inherited the business from a family member. What will happen when you no longer have to wake up at 5 am as you have done for the past 25 years? What new adventures/challenges will you set for yourself?
2. **Obtain legal, financial, and other appropriate advice.** In this step, you map out your post-sale financial plan. What happens once the business is sold? Where will you place the sale proceeds? Will you deposit the funds in a bank? Will you invest in stocks? Will you buy another company? How will the sale affect legal matters? Have you considered estate planning?
3. **Prepare your family.** Selling a business can have an impact on your family. How will the sale of the business influence your personal life? Will you spend much more time at home? Will the family dynamics change? Do children or other relatives currently have a role in the business? Was such a role, or even transfer of the business within the family, anticipated?

Business Steps

1. **Improve the financial records.** Transparency is important for the potential buyer, so have financial statements audited if possible. For larger, more valuable businesses, the audit is worth the additional cost. For smaller businesses, where audits may be prohibitively expensive, it is important that the potential buyer can verify your records through due diligence, references to bank statements and point of sale records, or other means. Transparency reduces the risk from the buyer's perspective, makes for a smoother transfer process, and gives you the opportunity to clean up any potential issues (legal or otherwise) before marketing the business for sale.
2. **Develop your staff.** Developing your staff has the added benefit of reducing the business's dependence on you. Reduction of this dependence, so that the business can operate effectively day to day without owner micromanagement, is key to improving the chances of a successful sale and increasing the value from a buyer's perspective.
3. **Establish, implement, and improve systems.** Work on improving your company's systems and controls (financial, management, operational). This facilitates the transition process for a potential buyer, making your business a more attractive purchase. Incidentally, this attention to systems and controls is generally recommended as a way to improve operating results for the current owner, whether or not a sale takes place.
4. **Clean up the business's physical appearance.** Just like a clean and organized house sells quicker than an untidy one, clean and organized business facilities present well to buyers and make a positive difference.

Market Steps

1. **Keep an eye open.** Pay attention to what's going on around you. Timing is everything, and selling your business at the right time can make a big difference. Watch for selling opportunities that may present themselves at a moment's notice.

When it comes to selling your business, you can never plan too early or be too prepared.

Part 3.
BUSINESS FINANCE

Cash: The Lifeblood
of Your Business

The maxim "cash is king" is particularly relevant for the owners of private companies, who do not have access to the same sources of capital available to public companies. Today's financial headlines are a stark reminder that cash is indeed the lifeblood of any enterprise. For some businesses, cash requirements and cash management are relatively easy to understand and predict. For others, however, the ebb and flow of cash can cause great anxiety. Why throughout history have there been so many businesses that are profitable on paper but unable to pay suppliers and staff and meet their obligations?

From a cash flow accounting perspective, businesses collect and recognize revenues from one of two perspectives: cash based and accrual based. With cash-based systems, the goods or services are paid for immediately during the transaction, and there is no time lag between the transaction and the payment. With accrual-based systems, there is a time lag between the sale of a good or service and the collection of payment. In addition to the cost of financing the customer, there is a risk of nonpayment, even though the customer already has possession of the goods or services.

An example of a cash-based system is a grocery store: you don't leave the store without paying for the items purchased. Even if you pay by credit card, the grocery store collects payment from the credit card provider. Whether or not you pay your credit card obligation, the grocery store's revenues are not at risk.

A good example of an accrual-based system is any business that offers credit to customers. For example, a plumbing business may provide the service requested by customers and then invoice them afterwards. The company has assumed the risk of nonpayment as well as the cost of financing the customer's payable. In essence, if the customer owes the company $1,000, the company loses the benefit of having that $1,000 available for as long as that invoice remains unpaid.

Estimating cash requirements using the back of an envelope for a cash-based operation is fairly simple. First, you examine the operating statement (profit and loss statement, or P&L) and determine the average monthly cash needs.

Figuring Monthly Average Cash Requirements

By using one year's operating statement, the owner can forecast increased revenue in the future by plugging in the numbers and using the same expense control percentages (.593 and .296 in the example below) to find the estimated future monthly average requirements.

Operating Statement: January 1—December 31

Revenue	$675,000		
Cost of goods sold:	400,000	.593	$33,333 average monthly expense
Gross profit:	275,000	.407	
Gen and admin:	200,000	.296	$16,666 average monthly expense
Profit:	75,000	.111	

Total average monthly operating cash requirement: $50,000.

Estimating cash requirements for an accrual-based operation, however, requires the efforts of a good bookkeeper and a financially literate business owner/manager. It is difficult to overemphasize the importance of financial literacy, particularly for rapidly growing businesses, as it can be the difference between business success and failure.

Determining the Need for Operational Cash

A rule of thumb is that businesses should have at least 3 months of operating capital available in cash. Some businesses will in fact maintain a standby line of credit, which may go untouched for years. For cash businesses, a line of credit is a nice thing to have; for an accrual-based company, a line of credit may be essential.

It is always good to have a bit of liquidity. Murphy's Law is always lurking, and finding yourself short on cash is the most stressful situation a business operator can experience. Know what it takes to carry on operations and when it's time to be concerned—long before it actually happens.

First Steps in Financing

Let's step back and take a closer look at the basics of financing. The wrong amount of financing, of the wrong type, taken for the wrong reasons, at the wrong time can drag a business down as surely as too little capital. No matter where the money comes from, it takes knowledge and planning to make it work for you. To do that, you need to understand what type of financing you need and are able to secure.

Equity Financing vs. Debt Financing

Let's start with the basics: There are two broad categories of financing: equity financing and debt financing. Equity financing/investment shares in both the upside and the downside of a business on an ongoing basis, while debt financing obligations must be met irrespective of the business's level of success.

You should look at your firm's debt to equity ratio. How much do you owe, and how much equity have you accrued? If you have invested significantly in your business or have otherwise developed equity, you will be in a good position to attract capital investment from various sources at favorable terms. If, on the other hand, you have a high proportion of debt to equity, you may wish to proceed carefully with any further debt financing. In such cases, experts say the wiser course is to increase your ownership capital—your equity—in order to avoid becoming overleveraged.

Think It Through

First ask whether or not your business really needs external capital. Is it possible to find savings through improved business operations or to more effectively manage existing cash flow?

If you determine that external financing is in fact needed, take the time to assess the situation from the perspective of a potential lender or investor.

If you were in their shoes, would you give financing to the business? If so, at what price? Questions to consider include:

- Is the business likely to repay the lender or investor an appropriate return for the associated risk?
- What exactly are the business's needs? Is the borrower looking to expand or maybe to build a cushion? In what specific ways will the money be applied?
- What is the borrower's level of urgency and timeline? Do they need funds to respond to a crisis or a squeeze, or are they planning to meet longer-term future needs? Keep in mind that the more urgent the need, the more a borrower may have to pay for that financing.
- What are the risks, whether unique to this business or the industry as a whole?
- How strong is management?
- How and how closely does the borrower's financing need mesh with the business plan? A plan that anticipates specific capital needs on the way to growth and success will speak volumes to prospective financing sources.

Answering these questions will give you a good sense of how capital sources will assess your business and will help you predict how much capital you will be likely to secure and how much it is likely to cost you.

Show Me the Money: Three Traditional Sources of Financing

The common hope when starting a business is that it will generate incredible profit, the business will become self-sustainable, its accounts will be swollen with cash, and the owners will retire into the sunset.

Before this can happen, however, the business's financial engine must be primed. This chapter discusses three traditional sources of financing: personal savings, friends and family, and bank financing. It provides tips for more successfully leveraging these financing sources and also considers some pros and cons.

Personal Savings

Instinctively, the first place that most of us look for financing is in our own pockets. How much money do we have in our piggy banks or under our pillows? When a venture is just an idea in our mind, we combine cash with 'sweat equity' to develop the business plan, educate ourselves about the market, and prepare ourselves. Those who are fortunate enough to have amassed sizable savings can look to finance equipment purchases, all or part of a business purchase, and more. The rest of us have to look to other sources as well.

Pros:

- **No external oversight.** You can spend the funds as you see fit without having to provide an accounting of funds, explain expenditures, or handle other administrative matters that might otherwise distract from your goal.
- **Fast turnaround with no bureaucracy.** Getting the cash is as fast as 'cashing in one's chips.' Maybe you have to withdraw money from a personal bank account; maybe you have to sell off an asset. There are

no forms to fill out, no wait for a committee; once the decision is made, it's full speed ahead.

Cons:

- **Limited availability of cash.** Few people have sufficient financial liquidity to personally foot all of a business's initial and ongoing financing needs.
- **No external accountability.** If you have no one to report to and are not required by a lender or investor to follow any specific processes, you are vulnerable to co-mingling of business and personal funds, lack of proper financial record keeping, and other mistakes.
- **Expense.** You may recognize the acronym OPM (other people's money). A generally accepted principal of 'cost of capital' dictates that when available and used appropriately, borrowing money or getting investments from external sources provides greater economic benefit than self-financing.

Friends and Family

This is when that football jersey you bought 2 years ago as a gift for your rich uncle becomes really important. Friends and family can add significantly to the pool of available funds. Several options are available for these individuals: invest cash in the company in exchange for equity, lend directly in the form of a personal loan, co-sign loan documents from an external financing source, and/or provide collateral to guarantee a loan.

Pros:

- **Perspective.** Friends and family will have followed your progress and when making the investment decision will have better insight into your reliability, strength of will, and other personal character attributes. This can assist in their decision about providing financing.
- **Nonfinancial contributions.** Some who become emotionally invested may also contribute access to their network of relationships, sweat equity, emotional support, and any number of less tangible yet important inputs.
- **Flexibility.** You should provide financial transparency with regular updates, keeping this investor group informed of progress, but they are usually more forgiving of miscues such as late payments. They are also less likely to require usurious rates of return on their investment.

Cons:

- **Impact on the personal relationship.** If not managed properly, the change in dynamics can negatively impact the personal relationship. What will be the new expectations and perspectives of the investor? Success of the venture may bring jealousy, and failure may bring resentment. Can these negative elements be avoided?

Banks

At this moment, somewhere in the world, a frustrated entrepreneur can be heard muttering some version of the old adage "Banks lend you money only when you don't need it and never when you do." Despite the challenges involved with establishing and maintaining a strong banking relationship, if effectively managed such a relationship can provide significant benefits. Options abound.

Pros:

- **Perspective.** The banker's perspective will generally be one of disciplined risk mitigation. Enforcing this discipline in the form of due diligence can encourage you to take a conservative approach and better prepare for possible negative outcomes.
- **Alignment of interests.** Lending is a key part of the consumer bank's business model. To put it succinctly, if they don't lend effectively, they will go out of business. By recognizing and leveraging this fact, you will benefit from the symbiosis inherent in the banking relationship.
- **Availability of cash.** Banks are the financial clearinghouses of the business community, and their lending reserves are sufficient to meet the needs of most business projects.

Cons:

- **Perspective.** Bankers are often seen as conservative. In their role as a lender, banks tend to focus more on the downside and figuring out recourses for negative outcomes. This perspective may conflict with that of the equity investor, who focuses more on the upside, and may be inappropriate for startups, high-risk ventures, or other opportunities that do not fit easily into the bank's assessment frameworks.

- **Red tape.** The level of due diligence required by banks, as well as the bureaucracy and methodical nature of the lending process, can be frustrating and cause delays.

Closing Advice

Some closing advice as you lay a foundation for future financing: keep feeding your piggybank, pick flowers for your favorite aunt, and breathe deeply.

OPEN SESAME

ATM

Banking Resources
for Growing Your Business

I
t has been said that "it takes money to make money," but few of us are born with the proverbial silver spoon in our mouths. For many business owners, a bank may be the first and most important port of call. Debt can be used to effectively weather difficult times, to help bridge the gap when growing the business, and as a financial leverage tool to create business value.

From the banker's perspective, effective lending and the provision of financial products and services is key to long-term success. The savvy borrower who builds a symbiotic relationship with the bank can obtain financial products tailored to suit his needs.

Types of Financial Products

You can benefit by appropriately using multiple bank lending facilities, including loans, credit cards, overdrafts, and lines of credit.

Loans

When assessing loan applications, bankers consider a variety of factors:

- **Creditworthiness.** This is your capability and willingness to repay—both as an individual and as a business.
- **The level of security or collateralization.** A loan backed by collateral—such as property or equipment, guarantors, stocks and bonds, inventory, insurance policies, or personal savings accounts—reduces the bank's perceived risk.
- **Type of business.** Banks consider current trends and economic projections for each type of business.
- **Financial records of the business.** Banks consider whether financial records are current and in order, where cash outflows made by the business go, and the status of paperwork and maintenance of records.

- **Whether the business is solvent and financially viable.** This involves an evaluation of the overall assets and liabilities of the business.

As long as the bank's risk/reward criteria are addressed, you can ask for flexibility in the structure of a loan. Negotiable attributes may include the following:

- **Collateralization options.** What level of collateralization is appropriate, and what should the source of any collateral be? Will the level of collateralization be adjusted over the term of the loan? When is collateral released?
- **Repayment schedule.** Is an amortized loan or a loan with balloon payments or irregular payments more appropriate? Is an interest-only period appropriate?
- **Interest rate.** Is a fixed or floating interest rate more appropriate? Is the proposed rate competitive?
- **Term.** What is the appropriate period of time over which this money will be borrowed?

Business Credit Cards

Credit cards provide access to quick financing for immediate requirements, without the administrative burden of conventional loans. For all intents and purposes, credit cards can be used as short-term unsecured loans. They may be used effectively for items such as travel and entertainment expenses, temporary cash-flow problems, etc.

Advantages include easy and convenient repayment, universal acceptance as a means of payment, and doing away with the need to provide collateral to secure funding. Credit cards often also provide incentive programs. On the downside, however, interest rates are steep and charges can pile up if payments are missed or delayed. Credit cards also provide limited access to capital, and credit card usage influences your credit rating.

Overdraft Protection and Lines of Credit

If you have an established, positive relationship with the bank, you may be an ideal candidate for overdraft and line of credit facilities.

Overdraft facilities can be effectively used by a business with fluctuating cash flow to smooth its cash position. For example, a building contractor who gets paid in installments and may receive a significant portion of revenue at the end of each project will need to have cash available on a weekly basis to pay employees.

Lines of credit can be effective for companies that import or export goods. Here, the bank acts almost as a trusted intermediary, with the line of credit representing security for both parties.

The Cost of Borrowing

The interest rate applied to a loan represents the direct financial cost of borrowed funds. However, you will want to consider a number of factors when calculating the 'true' cost of borrowing. For example:

- **Is the interest rate fixed or floating?** A fixed interest rate remains constant throughout the term of the loan, while with a floating interest rate the lender can adjust the rate based on market conditions.
- **How is the interest rate calculated/quoted?** Borrowing costs may be quoted as nominal interest rates or as effective interest rates. We will leave it for your banker to explain the differences, but it is important that you be aware because a borrower who thinks he is paying 10% a year in interest may effectively be paying almost half a percent more per year if the loan is compounded monthly.
- **What other fees/penalties are charged?** Additional bank charges may range from fees for loan origination and other administrative services to early payment penalties. (Yes, you may get charged a penalty for paying your loan off early!)
- **What are the opportunity costs of using this lender?** Do transparency requirements result in privacy concerns? Do the borrowing requirements impose restrictions that influence your business strategy or tactics?

Lending Covenants and Restrictions

Banks, like other lenders, must mitigate the risks associated with lending. In addition to screening potential borrowers and requiring collateralization, they will frequently attach specific conditions, known as covenants and restrictions, to the disbursal of monies. You should read the loan agreement thoroughly before signing it and seek professional assistance if necessary to interpret the terminology.

Typical covenants required by banks include:

- Insurance coverage for key management staff, property, equipment, or inventory against damage, theft, or loss
- The availability of books and financial documentation for inspection or audit by the bank or third parties at any time
- Preferential creditor status assigned to the bank over other creditors
- Bank's approval before any critical decisions are made on distributing profits, taking on new loans, or selling assets

Bank Borrowing: Some Pros and Cons

Pros:
- Convenience and access
- Variety of lending products offered
- Stability of the banking system, access to expert advice, and a continuous, steady supply of money

Cons:
- Conservative approach to lending, with less flexible rules and regulations
- Slow decision-making and administrative processes
- Restrictive covenants attached to disbursal of monies, with oversight that may be frustrating for the dynamic entrepreneur

Managing Your Banking Relationships

Recognize the importance of proactively building healthy banking relationships. Consider the following steps:

- Attempt to understand the banker's perspectives and concerns.
- Maintain regular communication with the banker; inform the bank of important business developments.
- Be transparent with the banker if/when issues arise. It may be better to forewarn the bank than to wait until the situation is dire.
- Develop relationships with multiple banks. Competition often results in improved borrowing terms and better service.

Closing Advice

Take your banker out for coffee and have a chat about how he or she can help you to be a better customer and what he or she can do to help you create value in your business. That coffee will likely be repaid many times over.

Part 4.
SPECIAL CIRCUMSTANCES
IN THE BUSINESS LIFECYCLE

AND OVER HERE, SON, IS OUR DISTRIBUTION CENTER. OF COURSE, WHEN YOU'RE CEO YOU MAY WISH TO RELOCATE IT.

Keeping Your Business All in the Family

The steps involved in selling a business to a stranger can be tricky to navigate, but what if you plan to sell or transfer your business to a family member? Personal relationships bring an added layer of complexity. Perhaps more than one relative is vying for control. Perhaps nobody in the family wishes to operate the business, yet the family doesn't want to sell. Perhaps you and the family are quarrelling because you don't want to let go of the reins. It's no wonder that such a small percentage of family-run businesses get passed down beyond the second generation.

Nonetheless, if planned and implemented correctly, transferring ownership of your business to a family member can be a rewarding process. The positives are that this approach may allow you to keep the business in the hands of a trusted owner, to rearrange your lifestyle, to take care of estate concerns, and to provide an income stream during a full or partial retirement. With ample planning and preparation, you can hand down your business while minimizing family friction.

Preparing Your Family

You should start to think about an exit strategy from the moment that you first open your doors. If you're thinking about passing your business down, you should consider grooming children from a relatively early age. Get them involved with small tasks like cleaning, stocking inventory or filing, and running errands. As they mature, increase the level of responsibility and sense of ownership. Explain more of the intricacies of the business to them, and begin showing them the value of their efforts to the business. As an added bonus, this early mentoring process will make a future transition easy for clients and staff as they get to know and bond with the future owners well before any ownership transition.

One important consideration is that children may have alternative life plans, and it is dangerous to assume that they'll have the same passion for the business as you. Give them the opportunity to get a broad education.

A solid business or industry-specific education will be valuable down the road for your business, but it will also give them the opportunity to make their own decisions.

Avoiding Family Friction

Here are some important tips to consider that can help avoid or at least minimize conflict during succession:

- **Recognize and accept differences.** Your heirs may have different management styles, different approaches, and different plans for the business. They may even want to be involved in the business in a different role than you had originally envisioned.
- **Take experience and personality into consideration.** Your heirs can run into potential problems if they don't have the necessary experience or haven't established strong relationships with employees and customers.
- **More than one heir? Consider what is equitable/appropriate.** For estate purposes, consider the value of different assets that will be passed down. This may require getting a business valuation done and even in some cases having the heir who is taking over the business paying money back into the estate.

Preparing the Business for Succession

Once you have a successor (or successors) in mind, it is time to think about your transition plan. Two major questions should be kept in mind:

1. **How will you transfer shares?** The next chapter discusses buy-sell agreements. Such an agreement can be used to establish the framework of the succession and the means by which the shares will be transferred. Consideration should also be given to the issuance of two types of shares—shares with voting rights for your successor and shares without voting rights for other family members not involved in the business or part of management.
2. **What are your tax options?** We recommend getting input from a qualified accountant or financial planner, versed in tax law.

Keeping your business all in the family may initially seem like an ideal plan. With careful, proactive planning and the support of a solid team of professionals, you can make succession a smooth process.

FINISH
LINE →

Buy-Sell Agreements:
How to Avert Disaster
in Your Business Partnership

One of the earliest decisions you'll have to make is how to build your team. Should you run the business on your own or take on partners? There are strong arguments for and against partnering with others and sharing equity; however, this chapter focuses on a different aspect of partnerships that many don't consider—until it's too late. While partnerships are almost always formed with the best of intentions, it is important to have a mutually agreed framework for ending the business relationship *before* it is needed.

If you have made the decision to set up a multiple shareholder business, consider the following scenarios.

Scenario 1: A dispute arises between two business partners, and one partner wants out. The controlling shareholder restricts dividends and other income that could be derived from the business investment.

The challenges:

- With the contentious nature of the relationship, how can the partners agree on an appropriate process for buying out the shares?
- How are the rights of the minority (non-controlling) shareholder protected?
- Can an agreement be reached without the threat of litigation, significant legal costs, and further ill will?

Scenario 2: One of several partners in a privately held business dies unexpectedly. Her estate must be settled, with the value distributed according to her will.

The challenges:

- The surviving business partners either don't have the cash or are unwilling to agree on a price for the shares held by the estate.
- The surviving partners want to restrict any external purchase of the shares.
- The surviving partners want to force the sale of the shares, while the heirs want to retain their ownership stake in the business.

Scenario 3: A married couple is going through a divorce. The husband started a business with a business partner several years prior to getting married, and the court has decided that the value of the business gained during the period of the marriage should be considered part of the marital estate.

The challenges:

- Neither business partner wants the husband to sell his equity, as this will harm the business, but the husband has insufficient liquidity to meet his obligations as part of the divorce.
- Even if the equity were sold, the amount of compensation received is likely to be impaired by the need for a quick transaction.
- Without a previously agreed-upon valuation mechanism, the process of deciding hoe to proceed may result in further delay and drag out an already difficult divorce.

As you can see, the events that can adversely affect a business partnership vary widely, and the lack of predetermined terms for buying and selling shareholder stakes results in an array of challenges—all with the potential for disaster.

For these reasons, a buy-sell agreement is of the utmost importance in any business partnership.

What Is a Buy-Sell Agreement?

A buy-sell agreement can be thought of a prenuptial agreement for a business. Due to the uncertainty surrounding the timing and circumstances of shareholder exits (whether voluntary or involuntary), a well-constructed agreement will map out processes, contingencies, and dispute resolution mechanisms—before these triggering events occur. It is generally appropriate for all privately held businesses with multiple shareholders to have a buy-sell agreement in place—preferably before a partnership goes into effect.

A buy-sell agreement may have a number of benefits, including:

- Establishing a 'fair,' structured plan for a shareholder exit.
- Enabling a smoother transition while normal business operation continues.
- Creating liquidity and a ready market to sell a business interest. Exiting shareholders are more certain of being able to "cash out" of their equity positions. In jurisdictions where there is a limited pool of buyers, this can be critical!
- Mapping out the events that will trigger the buy-sell. This helps eliminate ambiguity and reduces the likelihood of possible disputes.
- Providing procedures for dispute resolution, which removes emotion from the decision-making process.
- Predetermining the process by which the business interest will be valued, which will save both time and money when a shareholder needs to sell his or her stake.
- Assigning a value to the business interest without necessitating a purchase/sale transaction, which is particularly important in divorce scenarios!
- Protecting against unwanted new partners, which provides incumbent shareholders with an opportunity to either increase or decrease their existing shareholdings.
- Determining payment and financing terms.

Addressing the Critical Issues of Your Buy-Sell Agreement

Your advisory team, with a legal, accounting, and entrepreneurial finance background, can help you construct a buy-sell agreement that is appropriate to your needs and circumstances. We recommend the following process:

1. **Choose the appropriate agreement structure.** The three basic types of buy-sell agreements are *repurchase agreements* (in which the entity buys the interest from the exiting party), *cross-purchase agreements* (in which one or more existing shareholders buy the interest from the exiting party), and *hybrid agreements* (which may allow the founder first priority to buy the interest and other owners or partners the second option to buy).

2. **Negotiate the major provisions**. The provisions are the meat of the agreement and outline how exactly a business interest will be sold and to whom.
3. **Determine value and price**. Map out how the business interest will be valued and priced in support of the provisions. Will a business valuation professional be used? Will a previously agreed upon formula be used?
4. **Determine triggering events**. What events will trigger the buy-sell agreement? These can include death, long-term disability, voluntary or involuntary termination, or third-party actions, such as personal bankruptcy or divorce.
5. **Choose how the buy-sell will be funded**. How will the exiting party be paid for his or her business interest? Will it be an all-cash transaction, or can the transaction be financed? What insurance needs should be considered in order to provide immediate cash without causing financial harm to the company?

With all of the potential challenges of having a multiple shareholder business, you must be well prepared. It is important to have a well-constructed buy-sell agreement in place in order to protect your interests, as well as those of your partners. However, if like many private companies, yours does not have a buy-sell agreement, don't worry—you can have one created at any time in the business lifecycle. Should a dispute or other unforeseen event arise, you'll be relieved you did.

Divorce and Your Business: Working Towards the Best Outcome

D ivorce is not a pleasant topic, but unfortunately it can and does happen. We have heard anecdotes of divorces that have been made unnecessarily expensive, acrimonious, and difficult by spouses fighting over a business. It need not be that way.

Choosing a Path Forward

Three basic paths for handling a business during divorce are:

1. **Both parties retain equity ownership in the business.** If both spouses worked in the business prior to divorce, it may be possible to continue a working relationship despite the divorce. Even though the romantic relationship did not work, the business relationship may work. However, where there is rancor, continued joint ownership can be a recipe for strife.
2. **Sell the business and divide the profits.** This method allows both parties to extract cash. In practice, however, most private businesses cannot be easily sold under duress for a 'fair' price. It can take a long time to find a buyer, and this delay will require one spouse to run the business until it's sold.
3. **One spouse keeps the business and offsets a portion of its value with other assets.** This is usually the preferred option, assuming that there are other assets to complete the transaction.

The Legal Process

The court and legal advisors will be familiar with the conventional scenario in which one or both spouses are earning salaries. The marital estate may contain fairly liquid investment assets such as stocks or bonds, and there may be an ownership interest in a home. Here, the court can more easily make a decision on how to appropriately allocate the marital assets, while taking spousal support, child support, and related issues into consideration. Things tend to become more complicated when a business interest is involved.

Yours/Mine vs. Ours

A business started during marriage with investment from both spouses (financial equity, sweat equity) is often considered part of the marital estate (community property). A business that was already in operation or was begun with separate investment can be more complex to consider. The community interest may involve joint funds used to expand the business and any appreciation attributed to that contribution. If both spouses played a role in the operation, the contribution of each spouse must be considered. Even if no joint funds are contributed, a marital interest may exist and should be reviewed by a legal professional. To determine community property vs. separate property, consider these key elements:

- The source of funds for the startup of the business
- The date of the marriage (before or after the start of the business)
- The date of valuation—which can be either the date of separation, the date of filing, the date of the hearing, or some other agreed-upon date
- The contribution of each spouse to the business

A Cautionary Tale

The divergence of the estimated value of the business significantly increases when only one of the spouses is actively involved in the business. Some nonworking spouses mistakenly rely on the estimate of the working spouse because of a fear that the cost of a valuation may be prohibitive. The following frequently cited case from Minnesota illustrates the importance of obtaining an independent divorce business valuation.

Debra Sax married Paul Taunton in 1994. Taunton was the owner of a business called Athletic Fitters, Inc. (AFI). Taunton told Sax that the business was worth $6 million and his annual salary was about $300,000.

Sax filed for divorce in 1997. Both parties wanted to divide the marital assets quickly. Sax agreed to a divorce settlement based on what Taunton had told her about the value of the business and his yearly income.

Taunton had underrepresented both the value of the business and his personal income. A few months after the divorce was finalized, Taunton sold AFI for $30 million. A post-divorce investigation revealed that Taunton's annual income had been about $900,000 in 1994 and $4 million in 1996.

Sax sued Taunton's attorney, claiming that the attorney's firm had misrepresented the facts of the case. Legal experts did not expect Sax to win her case since Sax chose not to have an independent divorce business valuation conducted and relied on information provided by Taunton and his attorney.

Three Tips for Success

- **Mutual retention.** The valuation professional should ideally be mutually retained (hired by both parties). Both parties may choose to share the cost of a joint appraisal, rather than each person retaining his or her own expert. This course of action tends to save time and reduce concerns of bias.
- **Ensure transparency.** The valuation professional needs transparency and access to information in order to assist in an efficient and effective manner. The divorcing parties as well as their legal representatives should ensure that the business appraiser receives a complete perspective of the business's operations and financial history.
- **Appropriate use of valuation methodology.** The valuation professional must use methodology appropriate to the context of the valuation, the purpose of the valuation, and the unique attributes of the business. Valuation methods used when estimating the value of a business for sale may be inappropriate in the context of divorce or litigation.

While divorce is never easy (especially when a business is at stake), it can be made less difficult when the parties involved take a common-sense approach to the separation of business assets.

Note: This article is not intended to provide legal advice. We strongly recommend that you obtain assistance from a qualified legal professional.

ESOPs: When Sharing the Wealth Makes Sense

A major challenge for business owners is the hiring, attraction, and retention of quality employees. One solution that could be appropriate for larger private companies, but which you may be unaware of, is the establishment of ESOPs. The term *ESOP* doesn't refer to an ancient Greek storyteller but rather to an employee stock ownership program—i.e., a mechanism for 'sharing the pie' to make it bigger.

ESOPs are remuneration plans that businesses can offer employees as part of their compensation. In addition to allowing employees to benefit directly in the upside results of the company, ESOPs have the added benefit of increasing liquidity for business owners. So, what does that mean in plain language? Simply put, ESOPs allow you to sell part of your business to employees and buy it back later. In many ways, partnership structures in legal, accounting, and other professional service firms share ESOP attributes.

To establish an ESOP, the company can set up a trust into which it either contributes equity (shares) or cash to buy existing shares. Allotments of shares are allocated to individual employee accounts, and allotment size can be determined by a combination of criteria including tenure, level of pay, level of responsibility, etc. Graduated vesting of shares is a useful practice for further encouraging employee retention. With graduated vesting, the employee benefits over time from an increasing proportion of their allocation, based on the amount of time they have participated in the program.

While employed by the company, employees receive the dividends commensurate to their level of stock. Depending on the rights assigned to the shares, employees may also have some level of 'ownership control' over the direction of the company. When employees leave, the company must buy back their allocation (which is sometimes done in installments). The value of this stock can be calculated either by using a predetermined formula or by using the assistance of a valuation professional.

Determining Whether an ESOP Is Appropriate for Your Business

ESOPs are powerful vehicles to assist owners with transferring part or all of their businesses. Before deciding to implement, several points should be considered:

- **Up-front costs.** As with any benefit plan, it takes money to set up an ESOP, and often this plan has more up-front costs than other benefit packages.
- **Ongoing expenses.** Once it is established, an ESOP isn't much good unless the company can afford to make contributions. Are you willing to forego some discretionary spending in order to acquire the shares the ESOP needs?
- **Contributions vs. payroll.** There are practical limits to how much can be spent on an ESOP. Do you have a retiring owner who wants to sell millions of dollars' worth of shares to the plan? Make sure the company's payroll is big enough that the necessary expenditures can be made within the ESOP's rules.
- **Is everyone on board?** There isn't much point in having an ESOP if employees aren't interested in investing in the company. Similarly, if management or the partners aren't ready for employees to take an ownership stake, that could lead to morale problems. Make sure there's general support for the plan before establishing it.

Setting up an ESOP

Once you determine that an ESOP is both appropriate and feasible for your business, you will have to take specific action.

- **Find out what your company is worth.** A valuation is an essential tool for any business considering an ESOP. It gives a realistic picture of share value, which is what drives an ESOP. If the opinion of value were too low, who would sell to the plan? If it's too high, could the company afford a buy-back?
- **Determine a funding strategy.** ESOPs are flexible in that they can be funded through a number of methods including loans, direct contributions from company accounts, and even transfer of money from certain other benefit plans. Each has advantages and disadvantages that should be studied thoroughly.
- **Get professional help during set-up.** In addition to retaining a valuation professional, you should retain an attorney who specializes

in ESOPs to assist with drafting the language of your agreement. As with any financial instrument, an experienced lawyer is the best way to make sure your company doesn't accidentally miss any of its legal obligations. A trustee must also be named to help provide direction. The most immediate task of the trustee is to encourage participation by as many qualified employees as possible, because an ESOP only works if eligible participants actually participate.

Three Reasons to Implement an ESOP

Positive Effect on Employees

From the owner's perspective, granting employees the opportunity to hold equity can help to better align the interests of the owners and the workforce. Imagine that you're an employee who has a chance to become a partial owner of your company. Suddenly, you have an entirely new set of incentives. After all, you're buying shares at today's price but will sell them back when you retire or leave. Furthermore, the better the company performs, the better the stock performs—and the more money the employee realizes at cash-out. That's an even bigger enticement for good employees to stay on board and for all ESOP participants to find ways to increase share value. And when the fully vested employee does retire, there's going to be a natural market for those shares he or she is selling— the ESOP itself.

Additional Liquidity

ESOPs create a market for private shares of stock. By selling equity to the trust, business owners have the ability to either retain cash for operations or take cash out of the company without selling to outside parties. Business owners can thus gain liquidity without surrendering to the influence and demands of either financing sources or new external shareholders. When an owner leaves the business and needs to divest stock, an ESOP also provides a ready buyer for the outstanding shares and may actually be the first step to a management buyout. This can be particularly important for minority shareholders, who might otherwise be unable to induce their partners to buy the shares at a 'fair' or established market price.

Tax Benefit

Bermuda workers benefit from a tax code in which they are not exposed to the hefty income taxes levied in many countries around the world. However, both companies and individuals are liable for deductions tied to wages and salaries, including payroll tax and hospital levy. Dividends, the remuneration available through an ESOP, can be distributed deduction-free to employees, creating an economic benefit for both employers and employees.

Three Reasons To Be Cautious About ESOPs

Shared Downside

If the company underperforms, even in the short-term, employees may become uncomfortable with the ESOP's lack of diversification. In a more extreme situation, if the company fails, employees risk losing the accumulated value of their shares.

Added Debt

Funding an ESOP requires adding leverage to the company's balance sheet. This can impact the company's ability to explore new opportunities, to borrow additional funds, and even to finance operations in the near-term. Even if the company has significant cash reserves, it might be painful to tap those when it becomes necessary for the ESOP to buy back shares of vested employees upon retirement or departure.

Transparency

An ESOP makes participating employees partial owners of the business. That might not sit well with long-time owners, who may chafe at the idea of employees having access to annual reports, annual meetings, and maybe even voting rights. This access to information can impact salary and other compensation negotiations and may also present a competitive liability where secrecy is key to competitive success in the marketplace.

The Bottom Line

A powerful tool and great incentive for employee performance and retention, the ESOP can be a boon to a business. With careful consideration and qualified oversight, it can provide distinct advantages.

APPENDICES

Appendix A: International Glossary of Business Valuation Terms

To enhance and sustain the quality of business valuations for the benefit of the business valuation profession and the users of the services of its practitioners, five societies have adopted the definitions for the terms included in this glossary:

- American Institute of Certified Public Accountants
- American Society of Appraisers
- Canadian Institute of Chartered Business Valuators
- Institute of Business Appraisers
- National Association of Certified Valuation Analysts

The performance of business valuation services requires a high degree of skill and imposes upon the valuation professional a duty to communicate the valuation process and conclusion, as appropriate to the scope of the engagement, in a manner that is clear and not misleading. This duty is advanced through the use of terms whose meanings are clearly established and consistently applied throughout the profession.

Departure from this glossary is not intended to provide a basis for civil liability and should not be presumed to create evidence that any duty has been breached.

Adjusted book value. The value that results after one or more asset or liability amounts are added, deleted, or changed from their respective financial statement amounts.

Appraisal. See *valuation*.

Appraisal approach. See *valuation approach*.

Appraisal date. See *valuation date*.

Appraisal method. See *valuation method*.

Appraisal procedure. See *valuation procedure*.

Asset (asset-based) approach. A general way of determining a value indication of a business, business ownership interest, or security by using one or more methods based on the value of the assets of that business net of liabilities.

Benefit stream. Any level of income, cash flow, or earnings generated by an asset, group of assets, or business enterprise. When the term is used, it should be supplemented by a definition of exactly what it means in the given valuation context.

Beta. A measure of systematic risk of a security; the tendency of a security's returns to correlate with swings in the broad market.

Blockage discount. An amount or percentage deducted from the current market price of a publicly traded security to reflect the decrease in the per share value of a block of those securities that is of a size that could not be sold in a reasonable period of time given normal trading volume.

Business. See *business enterprise.*

Business enterprise. A commercial, industrial, service, or investment entity, or a combination thereof, pursuing an economic activity.

Business valuation. The act or process of determining the value of a business enterprise or ownership interest therein.

Capital asset pricing model (CAPM). A model in which the cost of capital for any security or portfolio of securities equals a risk-free rate plus a risk premium that is proportionate to the systematic risk of the security or portfolio.

Capitalization. A conversion of a single period stream of benefits into value.

Capitalization factor. Any multiple or divisor used to convert anticipated benefits into value.

Capitalization rate. Any divisor (usually expressed as a percentage) used to convert anticipated benefits into value.

Capital structure. The composition of the invested capital of a business enterprise, the mix of debt and equity financing.

Cash flow. Cash that is generated over a period of time by an asset, group of assets, or business enterprise. It may be used in a general sense to encompass various levels of specifically defined cash flows. When the term is used, it should be supplemented by a qualifier (for example, "discretionary" or "operating") and a definition of exactly what it means in the given valuation context.

Control. The power to direct the management and policies of a business enterprise.

Control premium. An amount (expressed in either dollar or percentage form) by which the pro rata value of a controlling interest exceeds the pro rata value of a noncontrolling interest in a business enterprise.

Cost approach. A general way of estimating a value indication of an individual asset by quantifying the amount of money that would be required to replace the future service capability of that asset.

Cost of capital. The expected rate of return (discount rate) that the market requires in order to attract funds to a particular investment.

Discount. A reduction in value or the act of reducing value.

Discount for lack of control. An amount or percentage deducted from the pro rata share of value of 100% of an equity interest in a business to reflect the absence of some or all of the powers of control.

Discount for lack of marketability. An amount or percentage deducted from the value of an ownership interest to reflect the relative absence of marketability.

Discount rate. A rate of return (cost of capital) used to convert a monetary sum, payable or receivable in the future, into present value.

Economic life. The period of time over which property may generate economic benefits.

Effective date. See *valuation date.*

Enterprise. See *business enterprise.*

Equity net cash flows. Those cash flows available to pay out to equity holders (in the form of dividends) after funding operations of the business enterprise, making necessary capital investments, and reflecting increases or decreases in debt financing.

Equity risk premium. A rate of return in addition to a risk-free rate to compensate for investing in equity instruments because they have a higher degree of probable risk than risk-free instruments (a component of the cost of equity capital or equity discount rate).

Excess earnings. That amount of anticipated benefits that exceeds a fair rate of return on the value of a selected asset base (often net tangible assets) used to generate those anticipated benefits.

Excess earnings method. A specific way of determining a value indication of a business, business ownership interest, or security determined as the sum of (a) the value of the assets obtained by capitalizing excess earnings and (b) the value of the selected asset base. Also frequently used to value intangible assets. See *excess earnings*.

Fair market value. The price, expressed in terms of cash equivalents, at which property would change hands between a hypothetical willing and able buyer and a hypothetical willing and able seller, acting at arm's length in an open and unrestricted market, when neither is under compulsion to buy or sell and when both have reasonable knowledge of the relevant facts. (*Note:* In Canada, the term "price" should be replaced with the term "highest price.")

Fair value. The proportionate amount of the total entity value without regard to discounts to reflect a minority position (for lack of control or lack of marketability attributable to the minority position).

Forced liquidation value. Liquidation value at which the asset or assets are sold as quickly as possible, such as at an auction.

Going concern. An ongoing operating business enterprise.

Going concern value. The value of a business enterprise that is expected to continue to operate into the future.

Goodwill. That intangible asset arising as a result of name, reputation, customer loyalty, location, products, and similar factors not separately identified.

Goodwill value. The value attributable to goodwill.

Income (income-based) approach. A general way of determining a value indication of a business, business ownership interest, security, or intangible asset using one or more methods that convert anticipated benefits into a present single amount.

Intangible assets. Nonphysical assets (such as franchises, trademarks, patents, copyrights, goodwill, equities, mineral rights, securities and contracts, as distinguished from physical assets) that grant rights, privileges, and have economic benefits for the owner.

Invested capital. The sum of equity and debt in a business enterprise. Debt is typically (a) long-term liabilities or (b) the sum of short-term interest-bearing debt and long-term liabilities. When the term is used, it should be supplemented by a definition of exactly what it means in the given valuation context.

Invested capital net cash flows. Those cash flows available to pay out to equity holders (in the form of dividends) and debt investors (in the form of principal and interest) after funding operations of the business enterprise and making necessary capital investments.

Investment risk. The degree of uncertainty as to the realization of expected returns.

Investment value. The value to a particular investor based on individual investment requirements and expectations. (*Note:* In Canada, the term used is "value to the owner.")

Key person discount. An amount or percentage deducted from the value of an ownership interest to reflect the reduction in value resulting from the actual or potential loss of a key person in a business enterprise.

Levered beta. The beta reflecting a capital structure that includes debt.

Liquidation value. The net amount that can be realized if the business is terminated and the assets are sold piecemeal. Liquidation can be either "orderly" or "forced."

Liquidity. The relative ability to convert assets to cash or to pay a liability.

Majority control. The degree of control provided by a majority position.

Majority interest. An ownership interest greater than 50% of the voting interest in a business enterprise.

Market (market-based) approach. A general way of determining a value indication of a business, business ownership interest, security, or intangible asset by using one or more methods that compare the subject to similar businesses, business ownership interests, securities, or intangible assets that have been sold.

Marketability. The relative ability to convert assets to cash very quickly and at a minimal cost.

Marketability discount. See *discount for lack of marketability*.

Minority discount. A discount for lack of control applicable to a minority interest.

Minority interest. An ownership interest less than 50% of the voting interest in a business enterprise.

Net book value. With respect to a business enterprise, the difference between total assets (net of accumulated depreciation, depletion, and amortization) and total liabilities of a business enterprise as they appear on the balance sheet (synonymous with shareholder's equity); with respect to an intangible asset, the capitalized cost of an intangible asset less accumulated amortization as it appears on the books of account of the business enterprise.

Net cash flow. A form of cash flow. When the term is used, it should be supplemented by a qualifier (for example, "equity" or "invested capital") and a definition of exactly what it means in the given valuation context.

Net tangible asset value. The value of the business enterprise's tangible assets (excluding excess assets and nonoperating assets) minus the value of its liabilities. (*Note:* In Canada, tangible assets also include identifiable intangible assets.)

Nonoperating assets. Assets not necessary to ongoing operations of the business enterprise. (*Note:* In Canada, the term used is "redundant assets.")

Orderly liquidation value. Liquidation value at which the asset or assets are sold over a reasonable period of time to maximize proceeds received.

Portfolio discount. An amount or percentage that may be deducted from the value of a business enterprise to reflect the fact that it owns dissimilar operations or assets that may not fit well together.

Premise of value. An assumption as to whether a business enterprise or intangible asset will be valued in liquidation or as a going concern.

Rate of return. An amount of income (loss) and/or change in value realized or anticipated on an investment, expressed as a percentage of that investment.

Redundant assets. *Note:* In Canada, see *nonoperating assets*.

Report date. The date conclusions are transmitted to the client.

Replacement cost new. The current cost of a similar new property having the nearest equivalent utility to the property being valued.

Reproduction cost new. The current cost of an identical new property.

Residual value. The prospective value as of the end of the discrete projection period in a discounted benefit streams model.

Risk-free rate. The rate of return available in the market on an investment free of default risk.

Risk premium. A rate of return in addition to a risk-free rate to compensate the investor for accepting risk.

Rule of thumb. A mathematical relationship between or among variables based on experience, observation, hearsay, or a combination of these, usually applicable to a specific industry.

Special interest purchasers. Acquirers who believe they can enjoy post-acquisition economies of scale, synergies, or strategic advantages by combining the acquired business interest with their own.

Standard of value. The identification of the type of value being utilized in a specific engagement.

Sustaining capital reinvestment. The periodic capital outlay required to maintain operations at existing levels, net of the tax shield available from such outlays.

Systematic risk. In relation to the market, the risk that is common to all risky securities and cannot be eliminated through diversification. In relation to an investment, the uncertainty of future returns resulting from the tendency of a security's returns to respond to swings in the broad market.

Terminal value. See *residual value.*

Unlevered beta. The beta reflecting a capital structure without debt.

Unsystematic risk. The uncertainty of future returns, because of characteristics of the industry, the individual company, and the type of investment interests, that can be avoided through diversification.

Valuation. The act or process of determining the value of a business, business ownership interest, security, or intangible asset.

Valuation approach. A general way of determining a value indication of a business, business ownership interest, security, or intangible asset using one or more valuation methods.

Valuation date. The specific point in time as of which the valuator's opinion of value applies (also referred to as "effective date" or "appraisal date").

Valuation method. Within approaches, a specific way to determine value.

Valuation procedure. The act, manner, and technique of performing the steps of an appraisal method.

Valuation ratio. A fraction in which a value or price serves as the numerator and the financial, operating, or physical data serve as the denominator.

Value to the owner. *Note:* In Canada, see *investment value*.

Weighted average cost of capital (WACC). The cost of capital (discount rate) determined by the weighted average, at market value, of the cost of all financing sources in the business enterprise's capital structure.

Appendix B:
Recommended Resources

Books

Understanding Business Valuation
by Gary Trugman

This text thoroughly examines the 'art and science' of business valuation from both an academic and practical perspective. It is regularly used as a reference in legal proceedings and considered key to the business valuation professional's library.

Private Capital Markets: Valuation, Capitalization and Transfer of Private Business Interests
by Robert Slee

This may be the most comprehensive text on private capital markets. It is recommended reading for the owners and managers of middle-market companies (with sales of $5 million to $150 million) as well as their professional advisors—valuation professionals, lawyers, accountants, estate planners, bankers, etc.

How to Buy a Business
by Joseph, Nekoranec, and Steffens

This is recommended reading for the 'Regular Joe' looking to buy a business. Understanding the buyer's perspective as communicated in this book is particularly useful for the business owner who is considering or preparing for sale.

How to Raise Capital: Techniques and Strategies for Financing and Valuing your Small Business
by Timmons, Spinelli, and Zacharakis

Whether you're asking your bank for a business loan or seeking help from investors, there is definitely a right way and a wrong way to request financing. *How to Raise Capital* gives you the real-world knowledge and perspective to help you prepare an effective loan proposal, find a suitable investor, negotiate and close the deal, and more.

Web

www.asgillpost.com
- Website and blog of Asgill Post Limited (the author's business valuation and advisory practice)

www.inc.com
- Website for *Inc.* magazine, which "delivers advice, tools, and services to help business owners and CEOs start, run, and grow their businesses more successfully." The 'Street Smart' series of articles written by Norm Brodsky is particularly recommended.

www.startuplessonslearned.com
- Although on the surface, this blog may appear to be directed to new businesses, much of the information shared is relevant for any business owner seeking to increase the value of his or her company.

About the Author

Kumi Bradshaw is a Certified Business Appraiser (CBA) and Business Valuator Accredited for Litigation (BVAL). He holds a bachelor's degree from Dalhousie University in Halifax, Nova Scotia, Canada, and an MBA with a focus on entrepreneurial finance from the F.W. Olin Graduate School of Business at Babson College in Wellesley, Massachusetts, USA.

Kumi currently serves as a member of the Accreditation Board of the Institute of Business Appraisers (elected in 2009). He is the valuations director at Asgill Post Limited (www.asgillpost.com), an independent business appraisal practice headquartered in Bermuda.

Kumi's business valuation and advisory experience includes assignments focused on small to mid-sized private companies in Bermuda, North America, and Central Europe. He has provided business appraisal (valuation) and advisory services for a variety of purposes, including buy-sell agreements, business purchase/sale, marital dissolution, shareholder matters, and exit strategy development. His experience includes the food service, construction, retail, information technology, health, child-care, and hospitality industries.

ASGILL POST

www.asgillpost.com

www.kumibradshaw.com

www.ingramcontent.com/pod-product-compliance
Lightning Source LLC
Chambersburg PA
CBHW060639210326
41520CB00010B/1662